Why Can't You See The Wind?

A Beginning Book About the Weather

By SALLY CARTWRIGHT

Pictures by WILLIAM PLUMMER

Editorial Consultant: MARY ELTING

WONDER BOOKS · NEW YORK

A Division of Grosset & Dunlap, Inc.

A National General Company

INTRODUCTION

Why do boys and girls ask questions? Mostly because they want answers. But sometimes they also want to wonder out loud. A question can tell as well as ask. It can tell about the surprising things that grownups take for granted.

And so this book was designed for children and grownups to explore together. We have called it a Beginning Book because it is an invitation to wonder and to begin finding out. In words and pictures it offers the youngest questioners a chance to think—and to discover some answers for themselves.

Library of Congress Catalog Card Number: 75-175631

ISBN: 0-448-04501-X (Wonder Trade Edition)
ISBN: 0-448-03618-5 (Library Edition)

How do you know the weather?
You can FEEL it.

Is it hot?
   Warm?
      Cold?
Wet?
   Or dry?

Can you feel the wind on your cheek?
Can you feel the wind
blowing through your hair?

You can feel windy weather.
In winter the wind makes you feel very cold.

How does it feel
when you walk in the rain?

Some people say
a rainy day is bad weather.
But some people
love the rain.

Stand quietly
in thick, wet fog.

How does that feel?

In winter,
how does snow feel?

Is it soft and light?
Or thick and heavy
and good for making snowmen?

How do you know the weather?
You can SEE it.
Look for sunshine and shadows.
Look for blue sky.

Look for clouds.
White and fluffy clouds
mean good weather.

Thin and wispy clouds
often mean that rain will come.

Dark gray clouds
almost always mean rain.

What do you see
in windy weather?
Look up in the trees.
Are the leaves shaking?

Wind makes ripples on the water.
Wind is air that moves
and pushes things.
You can't see it,
but you can see what it does.

In stormy weather
you can sometimes see hail.
Dark clouds and strong wind
often bring hail.

Look at the clouds in the sky.
Are they moving?
The wind blows clouds
across the sky.
What else shows windy weather?

Sometimes you can see lightning, too.
Lightning is fun to watch
from the safety of your house.

Sometimes in the morning
you can see dewdrops
on the grass and flowers.
People say dewdrops
mean good weather.

How do you know the weather?
You can HEAR it.

Can you hear the rain
on the window,
on the roof,
on the leaves?
Where else?

You can hear the wind.
It howls around the house
when you are cozy inside.

You can hear hail.
Hail is hard
because it is made of ice.
You can hear it when it bounces.

In stormy weather,
what is the loudest noise of all?
Thunder!

A storm brings
lightning and thunder.
Which comes first?
Thunder can be very loud.
But it never hurts anyone.

Some weather is quiet.
Can you hear snowflakes?
Snow makes a soft white cover
over everything.
Can you hear how quiet
the snow-covered city is?

You can see the weather outdoors.
You can feel it and hear it.
And you can MAKE some weather indoors.
Ask your mother to heat some water
in a kettle.

What happens when the water boils?
Do you see the cloud above the spout?
Your little cloud is made
of tiny drops of water,
like a cloud in the sky.

You can make a cloud
in another way.
Go outside on a cold day.
Blow your breath into the cold air.

Can you see a little cloud?
Tiny drops of water in your breath
make a cloud.
It is like the clouds
high in the sky.

The clouds you make
are also like fog.
Fog is really a cloud
that touches the ground.

Fog is made
of tiny drops of water.
When you go out in the fog,
you can see the tiny drops of water
on your sweater.

You can make a small wind.
First make a little flag
on a stick.

Then blow on your flag.
It will flutter.
Your breath shakes it
like the wind.

You can make a storm.
First make a little boat.
Use a paper cup.
Mother can help.
Crumple some paper.
Get a toothpick
and a square piece of paper for a sail.

Float your sailboat
in a pan of water.
Blow on it. Blow very hard.
What happens
when you blow a storm?

In a real storm
the wind makes big waves.
Boats hurry home.
In a big storm you hurry home, too.

When the sun shines again,
boats go out.
So do you.